D1024217

*Mother, you are just
too wonderful for words.
But I want to say this anyway,
because you deserve to hear it:*

*I love you
   and I always will
      with all my heart...*

*   forever.*

— Ceal Carson

Blue Mountain Arts®
Bestselling Titles

By Susan Polis Schutz

To My Daughter with Love on the Important Things in Life

To My Son with Love

By Wally Amos

Be Positive!

The Power of Self-Esteem

By Donna Fargo

I Prayed for You Today

Ten Golden Rules for Living in This Crazy, Mixed-Up World

By Douglas Pagels

100 Things to Always Remember... and One Thing to
Never Forget

Every daughter should have a book like this to
remind her how wonderful she is

For You, Just Because You're Very Special to Me

May You Always Have an Angel by Your Side

Required Reading for All Teenagers

Anthologies

7 Days to a Positive Attitude

Always Believe in Yourself and Your Dreams

For You, My Daughter

God Is Always Watching Over You

Hang In There

Keep Believing in Yourself and Your Dreams

There Is Greatness Within You, My Son

Think Positive Thoughts Every Day

For My Wonderful Mother

Words of Love and Gratitude

A Blue Mountain Arts® Collection

Edited by Gary Morris

Blue Mountain Press™

Boulder, Colorado

Copyright © 2007 by Blue Mountain Arts, Inc.

All rights reserved. No part of this publication may be reproduced, stored in a retrieval system or transmitted in any form or by any means, electronic, mechanical, photocopying, recording or otherwise, without the written permission of the publisher.

We wish to thank Susan Polis Schutz for permission to reprint the following poems that appear in this publication: "Since I had a mother whose…," "My Mother," "I Wish Everyone Could Have a Mother like You," "A mother should be…," and "You are a remarkable woman." Copyright © 1973, 1982, 1983, 1984, 1990 by Stephen Schutz and Susan Polis Schutz. All rights reserved.

Library of Congress Control Number: 2007903334
ISBN: 978-1-59842-194-1

▌▌ and Blue Mountain Press are registered in U.S. Patent and Trademark Office.
Certain trademarks are used under license.

Acknowledgments appear on page 92.

Printed in China.
Third Printing: 2010

✪ This book is printed on recycled paper.

This book is printed on archival quality, white felt, 110 lb. paper. This paper has been specially produced to be acid free (neutral pH) and contains no groundwood or unbleached pulp. It conforms with the requirements of the American National Standards Institute, Inc., so as to ensure that this book will last and be enjoyed by future generations.

Blue Mountain Arts, Inc.
P.O. Box 4549, Boulder, Colorado 80306

Contents

For My Wonderful Mother

When I was a child, I didn't
understand how hard you worked
to provide everything
you wanted me to have.
Some might say that's a parent's job.
But looking back,
I know you did so much more
and gave so much more
than you needed to.
And you did it with so much love.
You put your own needs aside
to care for me.

Now that I'm an adult,
I understand how you sacrificed,
and I know how lucky I am
to have been blessed
with such a wonderful mother.
I may not always say the words,
but I want you to know that
I love you and appreciate
all that you've done —
and all that you continue to do.

— Jason Blume

When I Look at You, Mother, I See Love and So Much More

When I look at you, I see my life through your eyes. I see the strength you always offer me, the comfort you continuously show me, the support you provide me, and the magnitude of the love that you unselfishly share.

I see the tears you shed when I cry, the laughter you share when I laugh, the hope you have for me when I feel disillusioned, and the faith you have in me when I face life's challenges.

I see the many sacrifices you have made and continue to make for me, the inspiration you are to me when I need direction, the devotion you show to me as a parent, and the encouragement you give to me when I need a friend.

When I look at you, and see my life through your eyes, I feel very loved, fortunate, and blessed. Thank you for being all that you are to me, for being the best, and for being more than a mother can be.

— Susan Hickman Sater

This Is a Story About a Wonderful Mother

This is a story about a mother who has the biggest heart in all the world. A mother who loves without condition and never gives up hope. A mother who offers all she can give and expects nothing in return.

This is a story about a mother who works so hard and does so much. A mother who never gives up no matter how big the struggle. A mother whose laughter can cheer up the world and whose smile can brighten a room. A mother who can mend a broken heart and chase the clouds away. A mother who is loved more than words can express and appreciated each and every day by the people lucky enough to know her. A mother who is a role model, an adviser, and a friend.

This is a story about you... the woman that does it all from the person who thinks the world of you.

— Elle Mastro

I Realize How Fortunate I Am to Be Your Child

I realize you had more important things
to do when I wanted you to
"look at me" or "watch what I can do,"
but you were always right there...
   praising me.
I realize there were countless nights
when you got very little rest...
because you were making sure
   I got all I needed.
I realize you could have said "I told you so"
a thousand times...
   and I didn't hear it even once.

I realize you are still the one
I turn to when I seek wisdom,
compassion, and love.
I realize your love and patience is what
made me the person that I am today...
    and I realize how blessed I am
    that you are my mother.
I can never repay you
    for all you've done for me...
but I hope that by sharing with you
a few of the things I have realized,
you will know how much I appreciate you.

— Eddy Rothenberger

Being a mother is a lifelong commitment
   to selflessness.
I think that motherhood must be
the most difficult commitment to pursue,
as more often than not,
it requires much more giving
   than receiving.
The rewards of this commitment
seem to be so very few,
and the demands so very great.

— Catherine I. DiGiorgio

Mothers are most likely
the hardest working people
    in the world —
yet they will probably never
    receive all the praise
        they are due.
In a way, this is easy to understand.

For how could words ever express
a lifetime of appreciation —
especially for a mother like mine
    who deserves the most gratitude
        my heart could ever hold?

Mother, I love you...
and I hope you know
just how special
you are to me.

                    — Barbara J. Hall

Mother,
I Will Always Love You

No words can describe the depth of my feelings for you.

Just the thought of you can bring a tear to my eye, a smile to my face, and the most thankful feeling I'll ever have... to my heart.

Your love is what sees me through more things than you'll ever realize. I cherish our closeness, just like I've treasured every generous, giving, understanding, and supportive thing you've ever done for me. The list goes on and on, and I'm not sure I could ever count all the things you've done that have made a difference to my heart and to my happiness.

The blessings that come from you are
the most beautiful things in my life.

There have been so many times when
you have felt just like a gentle sunrise
shining for me, sending wonderful wishes
my way, warming my soul, inspiring my
days, and lifting up my spirit.

You are just too wonderful for words.

But I want to say this anyway,
    because you deserve to hear it:

        I love you
            and I always will
                with all my heart...

                    forever.

                        — Ceal Carson

My Mother

For as long as I can remember
you have been by my side
to give me support
to give me confidence
to give me help

For as long as I can remember
you have always been the person
I looked up to
so strong
so sensitive
so pretty

For as long as I can remember
and still today
you are everything a mother should be

For as long as I can remember
you have always provided stability
within our family
full of laughter
full of tears
full of love

So much of what I have become
is because of you
and I want you to know
that I appreciate you, thank you
and love you
more than words can express

— Susan Polis Schutz

I Am Lucky to Have You for a Mother

In my growing-up years,
we went through so much together as
    a team.
You made my life your own,
sacrificing your happiness for mine.
You never gave up on me.
You simply stood by me,
reassuring me that I would make it
through any obstacle that came my way.
There were times when tears filled
    my eyes
and I was filled with doubt.

During those times when I was
    most fragile,
you were the steady rock that kept me
from falling apart.
You were so strong and loving,
so sweet and kind.

You've given me far more
than I ever deserved,
and I truly don't know
what I would do without you.
My heart is full of happiness,
all because of you —
because of your joy,
because of your love.
Thank you for all that you are.
I love you very much.

— Shannon M. Lester

As a Mother, You've Always Been There...

I came into the world and you were there to do everything for me.
I learned to let go of your hand when I took my first steps —
but I knew you still held me in your heart.

Those first steps put me on the path
toward my dreams and destiny —
but no matter how far they have
taken me,
I've always felt the light of your love
shining on my days.
Thank you for having a heart
so full of love that you were
willing to share with me.
Thank you for holding me close
no matter how far away from you
I may wander.
You're the brightest star in my sky —
and your love
will forever light my path
and always guide my way.

— Edmund O'Neill

You Are One of the Strongest Women I Know

Strong women are those who know the road ahead will be strewn with obstacles, but they still choose to walk it because it's the right one for them.

Strong women are those who make mistakes, who admit to them, learn from those failures, and then use that knowledge.

Strong women are easily hurt, but they still extend their hearts and hands, knowing the risk and accepting the pain when it comes.

Strong women are sometimes beat down by life, but they still stand back up and step forward again.

Strong women are afraid. They face fear and move ahead to the future, as uncertain as it can be.

Strong women are not those who succeed the first time. They're the ones who fail time and again, but still keep trying until they succeed.

Strong women face the daily trials of life, sometimes with a tear, but always with their heads held high as the new day dawns.

— Brenda Hager

A mother is the truest friend we have, when trials, heavy and sudden fall upon us; when adversity takes the place of prosperity; when friends who rejoice with us in our sunshine desert us; when trouble thickens around us, still will she cling to us, and endeavor by her kind precepts and counsels to dissipate the clouds of darkness, and cause peace to return to our hearts.

— Washington Irving

You Mean
the World to Me

Like a teacher's hand,
you guided me to do right.
Like a friend,
you were a shoulder to cry on.
Like an angel,
you watched over me protectively.
Like a doctor,
you healed me when I hurt.
Like a superhero,
you were the smartest and strongest of all.
Like the sun,
you shone your brightness down on me.
You will never know
how much you really mean to me.
I hope you are as proud of yourself
  as I am of you.

— April Aragam

The Greatest Gift of My Life… Is You, Mother

I don't recall the first time you held me
or when I first heard your voice.
But from the first moment
   you held me in your arms,
you made the most selfless choice.

You chose to change your busy life
   so that my life could begin.
You were my shelter from the rain;
   on you, I could depend.

You held my hand when I was afraid
and helped me to mend
my first broken heart.
You bandaged my wounds,
wiped my tears,
and kept me from falling apart.

You loved me without question,
no matter what I did.
You shaped me into a confident adult
from such an awkward kid.

Even though you're not always
right beside me,
your love is matched by no other.
And I'm thankful each day
for life's greatest gift:
having you as my mother.

— Stacey Swayze

Like No One Else...

My mother is a person who
believes in life's bright side.
I know, because she's helped me
to find it many times.

She is someone who considers
another's feelings first.
I know, because she's always
cared for mine.

My mother is a friend who will stop
    everything else to listen,
to be a special source
    of understanding,
and to offer hope and help
    in any way she can.
I know, because she's always
    been a guiding light for me.

I know how wonderful she is,
    but what I wish for
is the perfect way to let her know
    how much she means to me.

I love you, Mother...
and just thinking of you
has the power to
    brighten up my day.

— Barbara J. Hall

The Bond Between Mother and Child Lasts a Lifetime

The bond between mother and child
is a special one.
It remains unchanged by time or distance.
It is the purest love —
unconditional and true.
It is understanding of any situation
and forgiving of any mistake.

The bond between mother and child
creates a support that is constant
while everything else changes.
It is a friendship based on
mutual love, respect, and a genuine liking
of each other as a person.
It is knowing that no matter
where you go or who you are,
there is someone who truly loves you
and is always there
to support and console you.
When a situation seems impossible,
you make it through together
by holding on to each other.

The bond between mother and child
is strong enough to withstand
harsh words and hurt feelings,
for it is smart enough to always
see the love beyond the words.
It is brave enough to always
    speak the truth,
even when lies would be easier.
It is always there —
    anytime, anywhere —
whenever it is needed.
It is a gift held in the heart
    and in the soul,
and it cannot be taken away
or exchanged for another.
To possess this love is a treasure
that makes life more valuable.

— Stephanie Douglass

*F*or the mother is and must be,
whether she knows it or not,
the greatest, strongest,
and most lasting teacher
her children have.

— Hanna Whitall Smith

Women Who Change the World

There are women who make things better... simply by showing up. There are women who make things happen. There are women who make their way. There are women who make a difference. And women who make us smile. There are women who do not make excuses. Women who cannot be replaced. There are women of wit and wisdom who, with strength and courage, make it through. There are women who change the world every day...

women like you.

— Ashley Rice

Look in Any Mother's Heart and You'll Find a Million Memories of Love

A mother has an amazing memory
when it comes to her children.
She remembers the heartaches,
     the heartbreaks,
and all the love in between.
She remembers the accomplishments
and the delight in their achievements.
She remembers the arguments
and discussions,
the tempers that flared
and the tears that followed.
She remembers the sweetest hugs
and the saddest goodbyes.

A mother remembers the dreams
    you believed in
and all the things you did
trying to make them come true.
She remembers beautiful days
of watching you grow up
and become all you were meant to be.
She remembers how she changed
as life presented new challenges.
A mother's heart is full of love,
and it will never stop loving —
for she feels the greatest of all joys
in remembering a million different
    memories of love
she has shared with her children.

— Deanna Beisser

I think my life began with waking up
and loving my mother's face.

— George Eliot

My First Love...
My Mother

To her whose heart is my heart's
  quiet home,
To my first Love, my Mother,
  on whose knee
I learnt love-lore that is not troublesome;
Whose service is my special dignity,
And she my lodestar while I go
  and come
And so because you love me,
  and because
I love you, Mother, I have woven a wreath
Of rhymes wherewith to crown
  your honored name:
In you not fourscore years can dim the flame
Of love, whose blessed glow transcends the laws
Of time and change and mortal life and death.

— Christina Rossetti

My Mother, My Best Friend

I could not have asked for a greater gift in my life than to have you as a mother and a friend.

As I have grown, you have watched me experience all the joys and pains this world has to offer. You remained by my side every step of the way. You have always encouraged me, never doubted me, made me believe in myself, and never let me down.

You know me better than anyone else, and you're the first person I turn to when I need advice. You've listened to all my hopes and dreams: celebrating when they came true and comforting me when they shattered.

You have taught me life's lessons
and given me morals and standards
to live by. Your strength has helped
me accomplish so much. You have
handed me keys to open the doors of
opportunity. When one door closes,
I have the courage to open another,
knowing that no matter what lies
behind the door, I have your love,
support, and friendship to turn to.

You have exceeded the duties of a
mother and surpassed all expectations
of a friend. You have been and always
will be my best friend.

— Sherrilyn Yvonne

Only One Mother

Most of all the other beautiful things in life come by twos and threes, by dozens and hundreds. Plenty of roses, stars, sunsets, rainbows, brothers and sisters, aunts and cousins, but only one mother in the whole world.

— Kate Douglas Wiggin

You are a remarkable woman
who accomplishes so much as a
strong woman
in a man's world
You are strong but soft
strong but caring
strong but compassionate

You are a remarkable woman
who accomplishes so much
as a giving woman
in a selfish world
You give to your friends
to your family
to everyone

You are a remarkable woman
and you are loved by so many people
whose lives you have touched
including mine

— Susan Polis Schutz

If Not for You, Mother...
Where Would I Be Today?

I've been wondering
   about the precise time —
you know, the exact moment —
I began relying on my own judgment
and stopped relying solely on yours.
When was it that I started
seeing myself through my eyes
   and not just yours?

Exactly when did I gain
the confidence to trust myself,
   even when you didn't agree?
And how did you let me go?
When did you know my wings
   could carry me?

When did my dreams
    for my own life
take the place of
    your dreams for me?
When did you decide your job
    was done —
and it was time to step aside?
I don't remember when we became
    two separate people,
but I am grateful for the time
you let me share your knowledge,
    wisdom, spirit,
        and especially your heart.

I know now that though we are
    individuals,
I know I couldn't be me...
    without you.

— Lisa Crofton

What Is a Mother?

A mother cannot be compared to any other,
    for her love is ever-constant,
        unlimited, unchanging, and forever.
A mother will hold you while you cry,
    soothe you with kind words
        when it seems the rest of the world
        has turned against you.

A mother will love you when you think
  it's impossible that anyone could;
    no matter what you have done or said
    or failed to do or say,
      a mother truly forgives.
A mother will lift your spirits
  when you feel there is no hope,
    give you confidence and strength
      to begin again, and make you laugh
  when you think you'll never smile again.
A mother will stand by your side
  even when she stands alone;
    she will take you as you are,
      and never ask for more
    than your love in return.

— Flo Fessler

My mother was the most beautiful woman I ever saw. All I am I owe to my mother. I attribute all my success in life to the moral, intellectual, and physical education I received from her.

— George Washington

There never was a woman like her. She was gentle as a dove and brave as a lioness.... The memory of my mother and her teachings were, after all, the only capital I had to start life with, and on that capital I have made my way.

— Andrew Jackson

Mothers never change, I guess,
In their tender thoughtfulness.
All her gentle long life through
She is bent on nursing you;
An' although you may be grown,
She still claims you for her own,
An' to her you'll always be
Just a youngster at her knee.

— Edgar A. Guest

You never get over being a child,
long as you have a mother to go to.

— Sarah Orne Jewett

A Mother's Love Is...

A special kind of love that's always there when you need it to comfort and inspire, yet lets you go your own path. A sharing heart filled with patience and forgiveness that takes your side even when wrong. Nothing can take its place.

— Debra Colin-Cooke

A mother should be
strong and guiding
understanding and giving
A mother should be
honest and forthright
confident and able
A mother should be
relaxed and soft
flexible and tolerant
But most of all
a mother should be a
loving woman
who is always there when needed
You are a rare
and wonderful woman
You are everything
that a mother should be
and more

— Susan Polis Schutz

In Your Footsteps, Mother

I remember so long ago when I
followed so closely behind you...
you protected my every move
while holding my hand,
and your love never failed me.
As I grew from year to year,
your hand opened to allow my
reaching out and growth.
You watched me strive and achieve,
with so much pride and silent prayer.
You also let me fail on my own,
but were always there to pick me up
while we shared the tears.

Maybe words can never fulfill
just how much is in my heart,
but I want you to know that I've learned
so much from you, and silently
I will always reflect, with smiles
    and grateful tears,
upon our moments together.
I've realized that I may no longer
follow behind you as I did when I
was small; instead, our footsteps
have become equal strides as we
walk side by side, together in friendship.
I don't know if I can ever
repay you for the gifts of life.
But if I can live my life by giving
to others as much as you have
    given to me...
I will be following in your footsteps
    once again.

                    — Danine Winkler

Family
Is the Best Feeling
in the World

From it, we draw love,
friendship, moral support,
and the fulfillment of every
special need within our hearts.

In a family, we are connected to
    an ever-present source
of sunny moments, smiles and
    laughter,
understanding and encouragement,
and hugs that help us grow
    in confidence
    all along life's path.

Wherever we are,
whatever we're doing,
whenever we really need to feel
    especially loved, befriended,
        supported, and cared for
            in the greatest way,
our hearts can turn to the family
and find the very best
    always waiting for us.

                                — Barbara J. Hall

Tonight, Mother, I Remember

Tonight I remember
all the nights over the past thirty years
we spent together in your kitchen
washing dishes.
I remember the linoleum floor,
the white and yellow cabinets
so tall that I stood upon a chair
to reach the sink,
you in your bibbed apron,
and I with a dishtowel half my length.
I remember the first night,
so green to the task I broke a plate and cried.
You just laughed, making it all right,
and said in time I'd break a good many more.
You were right.
Tonight I remember hot August nights
when supper waited late upon
the man returning in the dark
from fields of new-mown hay.
Then, after everyone had eaten,
he trudged the stairs to bed,
while we two stayed to clear the dishes
in the stillness of the night.

I remember exhaustion
sagging down our shoulders
and collecting in the smalls of our backs.
I remember, too, your tired smile
and softly spoken "'Night,"
when the last crock was safely put away.
I cannot now recall all that we said
to each other over the years,
washing dishes after supper.
But I remember
nights we laughed together and cried
and philosophized and argued
and solved the problems of our lives.
Were it not for that daily chore,
that odious, routine task
(from which all others shirked),
I would not have these memories
and more, much more.
I miss those nights sometimes.
Even now, I miss washing dishes with you.

— Sandy Jamar

Our HOME is the place where I first learned to love and where I first learned to share.

Our HOME is the place where there is a person who always cares.

Even if I am far away, the memory of our HOME remains close in my heart.

— Andrew Harding Allen

A house is built of logs and stone,
Of tiles and posts and piers;
A home is built of loving deeds
That stand a thousand years.

— Victor Hugo

Thinking of home
Thinking of the past
Thinking of tomorrow
Brings me closer to you
You are a special person
who brings lasting joy
into my life

— Louise Bradford Lowell

If there is happiness in my heart,
    it's because you helped put it there.
If there is a gentleness in my beliefs,
    it's because you showed me how to care.
If there is understanding in my thinking,
    it's because you shared your wisdom.
If there is a rainbow over my shoulder,
    it's because of your outlook and your vision.

If there is a knowledge that I can reach out —
    and I really can make some dreams
        come true —
    it's because I learned from the best
        teacher of all.
            I learned... from you.

— Chris Gallatin

Since I had a mother
whose many interests
kept her excited and occupied

Since I had a mother
who interacted with so many people
that she had a real feeling for the world

Since I had a mother
who always was strong
through any period of suffering

Since I had a mother
who was a complete person
I always had a model
to look up to
and that made it easier
for me to develop into
an independent woman

— Susan Polis Schutz

Mother

The light, the spell-word of the heart,
  Our guiding star in weal or woe,
Our talisman — our earthly chart —
  That sweetest name that earth can know.

We breathed it first with lisping tongue
  When cradled in her arms we lay;
Fond memories round that name are hung
  That will not, cannot pass away.

We breathed it then, we breathe it still,
  More dear than sister, friend, or brother;
The gentle power, the magic thrill,
  Awakened at the name of "mother."

— Fanny J. Crosby

M is for the million things she gave me.
O means only that she's growing old.
T is for the tears she shed to save me.
H is for her heart of purest gold.
E is for her eyes, with love-light shining.
R means right, and right she'll always be.
Put them all together they spell "Mother,"
A word that means the world to me.

— *Theodore Morse and Howard Johnson*

20 Beautiful Things
That Are True About You

Mother, you are just the best... in so many ways ← You have a gentleness so gentle and a strength that few can match ← You work so hard and accomplish so much, and it's hard not to be inspired by all the things you do ←

For an angel, you're pretty good at providing the best down-to-earth wisdom I've ever heard ← And for a woman with a deeply rooted sense of home and family, you're very good at making things turn out just about as heavenly as they can be ← You are blessed with the kind of devotion that never goes away and with a great deal of encouragement that gets passed along ← You know when to be involved and when to let go, and you always know how to read between the lines ← You can give hugs that convey every thought and feeling to be shared, and you care better and more beautifully than anyone else ←

You are owed a thousand thanks for the smiles you give, the values you share, and the little miracles you manage to pull off all the time ⬳ I know the behind-the-scenes things you do never get enough recognition, but I hope you'll always remember that they are valued by me more than you'll ever know ⬳

I am so grateful I was blessed with you for my mother ⬳ I hope you never forget that ⬳ Thank you for absolutely everything ⬳ All my life, my hopes will stay strong and my sun will shine bright because of the love you have given me ⬳ Your enormous support and your unending love have been there always... in every moment, every conversation, every memory, and every glance ⬳ I hope you'll always remember...

All the wonderful qualities so necessary in a mother... are the things you possess in <u>such</u> abundance ⬳

— Douglas Pagels

My love for you, Mother,
is deep and unalterable.
In me, the memory
of your goodness and devotion
will never fade.
I should like to find words
to prove to you
how much I love you,
how my heart is filled
to overflowing with reverence
and gratitude
to you.

— Franz Liszt

*W*hen I think of your loving face,
and of how pleasant it is
to live with you,
of your deep serenity,
your charming tranquility,
I know very well that
I shall never love anyone
as much as you.

— Gustave Flaubert

*O*h, the love of a mother,
love which none can forget.

— Victor Hugo

A Great Mother...

Accepts and loves her children unconditionally.

Believes in each child's unique potential.

Comforts her kids when they're sad, disappointed, or hurt.

Delights in their successes, no matter how small.

Expresses her love in deeds as well as words.

Forgives her kids when they hurt or disappoint her.

Gives generously of her time, attention, energy, and money.

Hugs her children... often.

Intuitively knows what they need, even when they don't.

Judiciously disciplines with fairness and restraint.

Keeps things in perspective and doesn't sweat the small stuff.

Listens with her heart.

Motivates by her example, not just her words.

Never plays favorites.

Opens her home and her heart to her
   children's friends.
Protects her kids from harm, as best she can.
Questions and challenges them to learn and grow.
Respects them as they blossom into adulthood.
Supports them in their right to make mistakes
   and learn.
Tells them how much she loves and
   appreciates them.
Understands that parenthood is not ownership.
Vigorously works to teach her children good
   life skills.
Wipes away their tears and holds them when
   they cry.
Xtends a helping hand, even when her kids
   are grown.
Yearns to see her family happy, healthy, and strong.
Zings with joy to hear her children's laughter.

                                    — BJ Gallagher

A Mother's Courage

A *mother's courage is a powerful*
force. It is the courage that rises
up and declares to the experts,
"This child will not be left behind."
It is courage born out of love and
tempered by the heart's own song.

What courage lives in a woman who carries a child of uncertain capacity! How courageous the mother who flees in the night to lead her children to safety and shelter! A mother's brave heart will drive her to battle unthinkable odds on behalf of her offspring. She will lasso heaven and earth and move mountains to ensure that her child gets all he deserves. She will stand her ground in the face of relentless opposition and garner every resource to advance her cause. Her motherly might will topple laws and corporations, and serve as a beacon for mothers to come. When she's infused with love and on fire with courage, a battle against a mother will never be won.

— Rachel Snyder

If I Could Make the Perfect Gift Basket for You...

Inside it, you would find my heart:
one that is grateful for
the kind of person you are,
and for what you mean to me.
You would also find my memories:
a collection of thoughts and special
moments that we have known,
and of personal treasures
that only we two can share.
You would find many wishes:
for love and happiness,
health and prosperity,
wisdom and knowledge,
and pleasure and relaxation.

You would also find these promises:
that I will always
try to do my best in life
and follow my chosen path,
so that you can be proud;
that I will learn from my mistakes
and set a good example for others;
that I will always keep you close at heart
and regard you as mother and friend.
Around my basket of love
I would weave flowers and lace
to give it that extra touch.
Then I would deliver to you
this basket of love,
so that you could enjoy it
for years to come.

— Kelly D. Williams

Thank You, Mother

How do you thank someone who has given you the moon and the stars? How do you explain the deepest feelings of the heart? What could you say when the words don't even begin to convey the gratitude? With so much to express, where do you start?

I could spend a lifetime searching for the right words to say to you. The perfect words would be filled with appreciation for someone who took me by the hand when I was little and who guided me on a pathway toward more happiness than most people will ever know.

The right words would tell you how dear you will always be to me for holding the ladders that reached to my own little stars, for catching me whenever I fell, and for always being there with encouragement, support, and understanding.

Maybe I'll never be able to find those perfect words, but that won't keep me from trying. All my life through, I'll try to express that sweet thanks with each little reminder and every big hug —
 because you give my heart so much joy and you give my life so much love.

— Laurel Atherton

I Appreciate You More Every Day

You always told me that I could be
anything that I wanted to be.
You told me I was intelligent,
creative, full of talent,
and that no matter what
I wanted to do,
I would be able to do it.

But what about you?
Has anyone ever told you
how wonderful you really are?
How the love in your eyes,
the tenderness in your voice,
the soft, comforting touch of your hands
have healed more wrongs
than any team of specialists could ever heal?
That the place you have created, our home,
is warm and full of life and love?

Has anyone ever thanked you
for the love and the care
you put into the hours of everyday life?
Those are special gifts and special talents.
They are not something that you
can be taught in school.
They are gifts of love,
gifts that I hope to possess someday
and be able to share with my family.

Every day,
I thank you silently for the wisdom
you have imparted to me.
I thank you for the values that you
instilled in me.
But most of all, I thank you
for loving me so much
that I can still feel it
deep within my heart.

— Lea Walsh

I Wish Everyone Could Have a Mother like You

When you have a mother
who cares so much for you
that anything you want
comes before her desires
When you have a mother
who is so understanding that
no matter what is bothering you
she can make you smile

When you have a mother
who is so strong that
no matter what obstacles she faces
she is always confident in front of you
When you have a mother
who actively pursues her goals in life
but includes you in all her goals
you are very lucky indeed
Having a mother like this
makes it easy to grow up
into a loving, strong adult
Thank you for
being this kind
of wonderful
mother

— Susan Polis Schutz

Mother,
Your Love Will Live Forever Within Me

You gave me life, nurtured and cared for me, and when you felt the time was right, you set me free. Through the years, never once did you complain or wish for things to be any different. You simply took your life in stride, no questions asked, embracing the happy moments along with the sad, accepting all things for what they were. That was your way.

I didn't always understand or appreciate everything you did. I was a child with my own innocent perception of the world. Now, as a grownup, I can reflect with such admiration and respect on the wonderful woman and mother you were then and still are today.

You stood with courage to meet the responsibilities that fell upon you and sacrificed so much for the love of your children. What you have accomplished is more than you will ever realize. When I think of all that you have done for our family and all the love you have so generously poured from your heart, I feel humbled. There will never be enough gratitude to offer to you or a means to repay you. But my heart will always be filled with the joy of knowing your love. It is the most precious gift I have ever received, for it is the one you have so wisely taught me to set free and share with others.

I love you for being a caring person, a remarkable woman, and an exceptional mother. This love that you have given will forever live within me. Thank you for being my mother.

— Debbie Burton-Peddle

What Does It Mean to Have You as My Mother?

I have shared a relationship with you since the moment I was born.

The bond between us is enormous, and though sometimes it's not perfect, it's something I can always count on when it feels as if everything else is falling apart.

I'm so glad that the universe in its infinite wisdom allowed me to belong to you — to be your child and your friend. More than anything, I'm so thankful to have been given the honor to love you and call you my mother.

— Pamela Malone-Melton

May You Be Blessed with All These Things...

A little more joy,
a little less stress,
a lot more
recognition of
your wonderfulness.

Abundance in your life,
blessings in your days,
dreams that come true,
and hopes that stay.

A rainbow on the horizon,
an angel by your side...
and everything
that could ever bring
a smile to your life.

— Mia Evans

Mother...

There are so many words
I could try to say to you
to let you know
how much you mean to me,
but really
the two most important feelings
I want you to know are...

"Thank you"
for all your love,
and
"I love you"
with all my heart.

— Deanna Beisser

You Work So Hard
and Do So Much

You work so hard and do so much.
And I know that you wonder
sometimes — if anyone really
appreciates the efforts you make on
all those uphill climbs.

Day in and day out, you make the world a better place to be. And the people who are lucky enough to be in your life are the ones who get to see that you're a very wonderful person with a truly gifted touch. You go a million miles out of your way and you always do so much... to make sure that other lives are easier and filled with happiness. Your caring could never be taken for granted because the people you're close to are blessed... with someone who works at a job well done to bring smiles to the day.

You're a special person who deserves more thanks than this could ever say.

— Jenn Davids

I Wish I Could Do This for You...

I wish I could make sure
   you always had the best —
like laughter, rainbows,
   butterflies, and health.
I wish I could take you anywhere
   you wanted to go
and treat you to waterfalls,
   rivers, forests, and mountaintops.
I wish I could make it possible for you
to do anything you ever dreamed of,
even if just for a day.
I wish I could keep you from
   ever being hurt or sad
and that all your troubles
   and problems would disappear.

I wish that I could package up
all the memories that bring smiles to you
and have them handy for
  your immediate enjoyment.

I wish I could guarantee you peace of mind,
  contentment, faith, and strength,
as well as the constant ability
  to find joy in all the things
that sometimes go unnoticed.
I wish you moments to connect
  with other individuals
who are full of smiles and hugs to give away
and stories and laughter to share.
I wish you could always know
  how much you mean to me —
because no matter what's going on
  in our lives,
you are loved and appreciated.

— Barbara Cage

You're the Very <u>Best</u> Mother of All

*T*hank you
for a lifetime of loving me —
for believing in me
and for putting my hopes,
my dreams, and my needs
ahead of your own.

You might think
that no one noticed,
but I want you to know
how deeply you are appreciated.

I have a thousand memories
that I will cherish forever
because of the extra effort,
the special care,
and the love that
you always put into
all that you do.

Thank you for being
the very best mother in the world.

— Jason Blume

ACKNOWLEDGMENTS

We gratefully acknowledge the permission granted by the following authors and authors' representatives to reprint poems or excerpts from their publications.

Jason Blume for "For My Wonderful Mother" and "You're the Very Best Mother of All." Copyright © 2004, 2006 by Jason Blume. All rights reserved.

Eddy Rothenberger for "I Realize How Fortunate I Am to Be Your Child." Copyright © 2007 by Eddy Rothenberger. All rights reserved.

Deanna Beisser for "Look in Any Mother's Heart and You'll Find a Million Memories of Love." Copyright © 2007 by Deanna Beisser. All rights reserved.

Lisa Crofton for "If Not for You, Mother... Where Would I Be Today?" Copyright © 2007 by Lisa Crofton. All rights reserved.

Sandy Jamar for "Tonight, Mother, I Remember." Copyright © 2007 by Sandy Jamar. All rights reserved.

BJ Gallagher for "A Great Mother...." Copyright © 2007 by BJ Gallagher. All rights reserved.

Rachel Snyder for "A Mother's Courage." Copyright © 2007 by Rachel Snyder. All rights reserved.

A careful effort has been made to trace the ownership of selections used in this anthology in order to obtain permission to reprint copyrighted material and give proper credit to the copyright owners. If any error or omission has occurred, it is completely inadvertent, and we would like to make corrections in future editions provided that written notification is made to the publisher:

BLUE MOUNTAIN ARTS, INC., P.O. Box 4549, Boulder, Colorado 80306.